Acknowledgement

This book is dedicated to our friends and families. Thank you for cultivating our playful imaginations, providing an oasis for laughter and fun, and teaching us that life is indeed better with the shared comforts of friends, family...and furry creatures.

Donna & Diana

Introduction

Our feline friends touch our lives in unexpected ways. They generate excitement around every turn and give us an insight into their world—and perhaps our world too.

As cat admirers, we couldn't help but wonder what these champions of charm would share if they could speak their minds. So we went on a journey to find out. We hope you enjoy the thoughts, stories, facts, and humor we discovered.

If My Cat Could Talk...

by Donna Hershfeldt
and Diana Losacco

Typography by Design Dynamic

Published by Great Quotations Inc.
8102 Lemont Road, #300
Woodridge, IL 60517

ISBN 1-56245-495-1

Printed in Hong Kong 2004

Thousands of years ago cats were worshipped as gods. Cats have never forgotten this.

—Anonymous

Just try me

- I've never been known as "Man's Best Friend"

- I don't always show affection in ways you'd comprehend

- But if you get to know me I think I can say

- I'll give you lots of love in my special feline way!

WE'RE INSTINCTIVELY WILD

BUT DOMESTICALLY MILD!

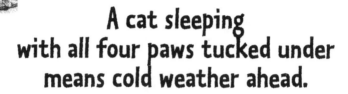

A cat sleeping
with all four paws tucked under
means cold weather ahead.

—English superstition

So why can't the weatherman
get it right?

**A Texas Tabby
had more than 420 kittens before
having her last litter at age 18!**

Guess everything IS bigger in Texas...

A Cat By Any Other Name Is Still A Cat

- In English, cat is "cat"

- Cat is "chat" in French and "katze" in German

- The Spanish word for cat is "gato"

- The Italians pronounce it "gatto"

- We are "neko" in Japanese

- Arabic countries call us "kitte"

Let me tell you, though, we cats have been called some other names...

Words from little friends...

"I like my cat because he lets me read stories to him and because he hasn't died yet and because he gets to sleep in the garage and I don't get to."

Austin
Age: 4
Cat: "Socks"

Happy is the home
with at least one cat.

—Italian Proverb

How's your vocatulary?

CATASTROPHIC = What happens when our owners leave us cats for too long

CATALYST = A list of our favorite tuna brands

COPYCAT = Dogs that try to be more like us cool cats

CATACOMB = A soft comb used to groom us gorgeous long-haired cats

KATMANDO = An owner who does everything we train him to do

Cat Fact

Cats have five toes on each front paw but only four toes on each back paw.

It throws the girls at the nail salon every time!

CAT YEARS

We cats don't care much for math, but we're always being asked about this human-versus-cat age thing. It goes like this:

If I'm 3, then I'm 21 human years old.

If I'm 8, I'm 40 human years old.

If I'm 14, well, the way I see it, I'm darn old!

Cat Fact

Let sleeping cats lie!

We cats sleep through half our lives. Our sleeping consists of about 70 percent in light sleep and the rest in deep sleep. But who cares about light or deep; just help me find that perfectly warm, cozy place to plop down and catch some ZZZs!

So have you ever known us cats to need sleeping pills?

Words from little friends...

How did your cat get its name?

"Because that's what we call it."

Sonya
Age: 4
Cat: "Rover"

Cat Fact

PUMPIN' IRON

Did you know we cats have 290 bones
and 517 muscles in our bodies?

But we hope you love us for our
brains, not our bodies...

Black Cat

A cat as black
As blackest coal
Is out upon
His midnight stroll,
His steps are soft,
His walk is slow,
His eyes are gold,
They flash and glow.
And so I run
And so I duck,
I do not need
His black-cat luck.

–Anonymous

It's grrreat to be a cat:

- I don't have to seek out the next fad diet
- I do whatever I want, when I want
- I can stay out all night and sleep all day
- I don't have to pay taxes
- I don't have complicated relationships
- I don't have to deal with computers
- I don't have to wait in lines!

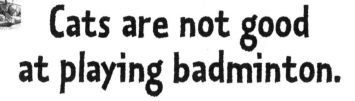

Cats are not good at playing badminton.

Where's the birdie?
Anyone seen the birdie?

Cat Fact

We cats come across as sweet and gentle,
but we really have a wild side.
As direct descendants of the WILDCAT
(the Felis Silvestris species),
we are divided into the African wildcat,
European wildcat and Steppe wildcat.

PURR! Uh, I mean, GRRRR!

Resting, Relaxing, Resting, Relaxing...
A feline's favorite thing to do

I'D LIKE YOU TO MEET...

When introducing adult cats to each other, two neutered males tend to resolve conflicts. However, females appear to be more territorial after maturing independently and may never settle their differences. Oh heck, just offer them the shopping network and everything should be fine.

I was so confused.
For years I thought my
name was "Shoo!"

We cats love
to sleep. Sometimes we even
dream.

And we love
counting mice to get
to sleep!

School Finals

- The Art of Toilet Paper Unrolling
- Litterbox Etiquette
- Purrsuasion Techniques
- The Language of Meowing, Yeowling, and Growling
- Introduction to Social Behavior (Dealing with Household Characters such as Dogs, Boyfriends, Girlfriends, Neighbors)
- Hissing 101

Failed again...

A kitten is
in the animal world
what a rosebud
is in a garden.

–Robert Southey
(1774-1843)

Cat Fact

Now really, have you ever seen it "rain cats and dogs?"

The saying, "Its been raining cats and dogs," originated when narrow city streets had poor drainage. During rainstorms, the rushing water would sweep cats and dogs down alleys and other pathways!

This might have started the river rafting craze...

CATERCISE

You may wonder why we apparently smart cats run in circles chasing our tails. It provides aerobic activity and allows us cats to keep our legs limber! Who needs Jane Fonda or Richard Simmons?

No one OWNS me!

I CAN'T HELP MYSELF...

I have this bad habit of, uh, finding things to sharpen my claws on. Recently, I, uh, found the couch, and, uh, shredded the bottom. I was glad my owners had a sense of humor about it. They just tell people it's the latest fringed look!

Words from little friends...

"My cat doesn't have a bed because he never sleeps. He just walks around all the time."

Aaron
Age: 5
Cat: "Frat"

Cat Fact

Splash! Splash! It's not true that all of us cats dislike water. A rare breed called the "Turkish Van" is known for its love of water. In their native regions they are known as the "Swimming Cats."

Surfboarding is out of the question, though.

When I was growing up,
I always heard,
"It's a dog-eat-dog world
out there."

Poor dogs.

It's time for the Feline Cable Network...

- The Dave Litterman Show   - Tomcat, P.I.
- The Tunanight Show   - Litterbox Living
- Allleycat McBeal   - The Purrfect Link

Get the remote, serve the catnip, make room on the couch!

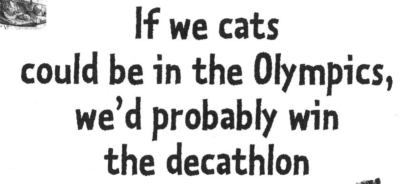

If we cats
could be in the Olympics,
we'd probably win
the decathlon

ON THE ROAD AGAIN

You've heard about us cats "unwillingly" moving with our owners.... There was one such cat that moved from Utah to Washington State. Shortly thereafter, he disappeared. One year later, he arrived back at his original home in Utah—over 800 miles away!

Guess he didn't much care for rainy weather!

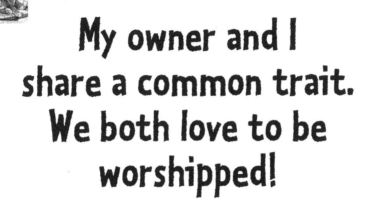

My owner and I
share a common trait.
We both love to be
worshipped!

Cat Fact

Men at sea believed tortoiseshell cats brought them luck. In fact, Japanese sailors carried a tri-colored cat aboard as they believed these cats could give early warnings of an approaching storm.

I wonder if the cats got to play poker with the deck hands...

CATS ROCK!

I'm simply Purrr-fect!

CATs are PHAT!

UNITED WE PURR!

CAT POWER

CATS IN HIGH PLACES

- The first White House cat, Tabby, belonged to Abraham Lincoln
- Rutherford B. Hayes had a Siamese cat named Siam
- President McKinley owned an Angora
- Calvin Coolidge had several cats
- Woodrow Wilson kept a cat in the White House
- Slippers was Teddy Roosevelt's cat

CATS IN HIGH PLACES
(continued)

- John Kennedy's cat was named Tom Kitten
- Gerald Ford had a Siamese cat
- Jimmy Carter had a cleverly named Siamese cat: Misty Malarky Ying Yang
- Bill Clinton had "Socks" the cat
- The George W. Bushes have two cats named Ernie and India

By the way, it's politically correct to lobby us for attention!

Cats rule!
And speaking of rules,
I make my own!

You might think acting is hard work, but it comes naturally to us cats. Just ask my agent.

Stunt cats have strutted their stuff on the big screen for years. Twelve cats were used for the movie, "Harry Potter and the Philosopher's Stone." And they were given the royal treatment! Rumor has it each cat got their own room, whatever food they wanted and fur-lined baskets!

I'm off to Hollywood...

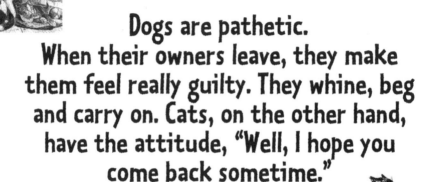

Dogs are pathetic.
When their owners leave, they make
them feel really guilty. They whine, beg
and carry on. Cats, on the other hand,
have the attitude, "Well, I hope you
come back sometime."

NOW THAT'S OLD!

One of the oldest cats on record lived to be 36 years old!

Humm, I want to know what the owner fed that cat...

Cats bring sunshine
to a home. By the time we
come home,
it's usually morning!

We cats are pros at patience.
In fact, we could be patience professors.
Do you know I've been known to wait for
DAYS for a potential prey?

Okay okay, so I'll admit it...
my patience skills just flat out leave me
when it's time for my daily
meal to be served!

My function is simply to be admired!

Cat Fact

Did you know hundreds of cats live in libraries throughout the U.S.? They're known as "library cats." In fact, it's believed there were cats in the Alexandria library in Egypt in 300 B.C.!

You'd think we cats would know how to read by now...

WELCOME TO THE ACATEMY AWARDS!

And the winner is...

- Crouching Tiger, Hidden Catnip
- Sound of Meowsic
- 101 Tabbies
- Cat Wars
- Silence of the Kitties
- Beverly Hills Cat

My owner accuses me
of being a cat with a split personality!
It seems like an unfair accusation.
Sure, I split about a year ago,
but I did find my way back home...

We cats are so unique that you'll find many words and sayings that use our name. Here's a few: Catnap, Catty, Cathouse, Kittenish, Catlike, Catty-corner, Letting the Cat out of the bag.

Now that's the Cat's Meow!

I'm easily entertained;
just give me a piece a rug.

We cats are often associated with symbols such as craftiness, magic, the moon, love, vision.

I personally associate us with magnificent, stupendous, your highness... What's the symbol for that anyway?

CAT HEROS

Let's hear a round of appaws for all my fellow cats who are brave and courageous!

– The cat who awoke owners when their child was taken ill during the night

– The cat who saved her kittens from a burning building

– The cat who pounced on burglars during an attempted robbery

– And the many hundreds of cats that alert owners of fire nearby!

Cat Fact

Just when you thought all cats were the same, think again!

Take the Burmese, for instance. These fellow cats are the most "dog-like" in their tendency to stick close to their owners and to give and receive affection. They also expect you to take care of all their needs. Because they are very trusting animals and have little survival instincts, they shouldn't be let outdoors.

Sounds like a pretty good line to me...

We cats try to find
owners with similar personality
traits. They must be self sufficient,
independent, intelligent, skillful,
seductive, playful, and at
times...slightly neurotic.

Cat Fact

I CAN'T SMILE; YOU CAN'T PURR!

We cats purr at about 26 cycles per second. Some claim it is the vibration of our vocal cords when we inhale and exhale. Others claim it is a vibration caused by blood passing through a large vein in our chest.

In any event, it beats tail wagging!

Hey, what's with the,
"Here, kitty, kitty, kitty"!
Kitty is NOT my name.
Of course, even if you called
me by my name,
I may not
choose to come.

Cat Fact

Did you know the ancient Egyptians worshipped cats as gods? In the 1800s, over 300,000 mummified cats were found in Egypt. Also, Egyptians shaved their eyebrows to mourn the loss of a beloved cat.

Bet you're glad that ritual has passed.

Cat Kisses

Sandpaper kisses
On a cheek or a chin
That is the way
for a day to begin!
Sandpaper kisses
A cuddle and a purr.
I have an alarm clock
That's covered in fur!

—Anonymous

Cat Fact

THUMP THUMP

A cat's heart beats about twice as fast as a human heart (at 110-140 beats per minute).

Guess we cats will never be accused of being "half-hearted" companions...

Hero Owners!

When everyone else gave up on me (including my vet who thought I had no chance), my owner believed I could make it. He tried everything to get me back to good health and miraculously came up with a cure—surprising even the doctors—and saved my life. My owner is one cool cat. Human cat that is.

Owner: Brian
Cat: Mikey

CALLING
ALL WHITE CATS...

Dreaming of a white cat means good luck.
— American superstition

To see a white cat on the road is lucky.
— American superstition

So if you see a bunch of white cats standing in line to buy PowerBall tickets, you'll know why...

Cat Fact

We cats specialize in sunbathing. But please don't forget that like you humans, we need sunscreen to protect our sensitive skin. Really.

But, PLEASE, don't make us wear THONG BIKINIs!

Words from little friends...

"I like my cat because she gives me kitty kisses. And I like my cat because she likes me."

Jared
Age: 5
Cat: "Kitty"

HERE IS AN ILLUMINATING BIT OF CAT FUN

A flashlight makes a great cat toy. Turn the flashlight on in a dark room and watch me chase the beam of light. Hey, don't laugh; I know of a certain species who chase a little white ball around. They call it golf...

CATNIP...
a cat's drug of choice!

When the cat's away, the mouse will play... but not after the cat returns!

Cats' popularity increased when our owners realized cat's usefulness for reducing the vermin population. This respect remains to the present day. What is a vermin anyway?

The CAT's PAJAMAS

No, we cats do not wear pajamas! If we wanted some pajamas, though, we would contact the Costume & Set Designer for the musical CATS. Now those are some fine cat dress-ups!

Did you know that CATS is one of the longest running musicals on Broadway and London's West End? It has won many awards (including 7 Tony awards in 1983).

I'm cool, I'm cool...I'm cool
BOO! Funny Halloween Costume

This Halloween Costume made even a serious cat like me crack a smile. The human had a stuffed cat sitting on top of her head. Her body costume was a series of scratch marks. The writing on the costume said, "Ask me about my cat."

Whew, her cat must have a major cattitude!

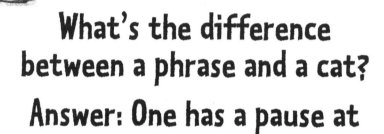

What's the difference between a phrase and a cat?

Answer: One has a pause at the end of its clause.

A strange black cat on your porch brings prosperity.
—*Scottish superstition*

And a strange black cat in your house may very likely cause calamity!

Cat Fact

Cat Olympians!

We cats have sharp reflexes and our spine is flexible, allowing us to squeeze through the tiniest of gaps.

And don't try to outrun us. When we run, all our legs are in the air for a time and we can accelerate up to 30mph for short bursts.

Was Superman actually a cat?

Dogs are really gross!

Cat Fact

A Bobcat is not a cat named Bob! (Or is it?)

The name bobcat is an abbreviation of "bob-tailed cat" and refers to the cat's short, dark ringed tail. The bobcat has been called the Red Lynx, Barred Bobcat, Bay Lynx and Wild Cat.

He probably got fed up with all the name changes and just decided to call himself "Bob."

Tomcat Corleone

In most hoods, cats have a godfather or "top cat." This dude has won the respect as the roughest and toughest cat. He stays at the top of the ladder until overthrown by a tougher feline. Some leaders stay at the top for years.

This power does not bring any mating perks, however. Oh darn! Unlike some other social animals, the cat leader doesn't always get the choicest females (a scroungy tomcat down the hierarchy may win out).

The WORLD is mine!

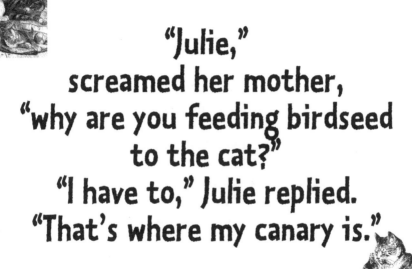

"Julie,"
screamed her mother,
"why are you feeding birdseed
to the cat?"
"I have to," Julie replied.
"That's where my canary is."

CAT FASHIONS

You want fashion? Just take a look at some of us cats! Admire the full pelt of the Persian. Or how about the very sleek and close-lying coats of the Siamese and Orientals? Or do you prefer the long, soft and silky coats of the longhaired foreign breed? And for those shoppers looking for something unique, check out the cat with "double" coats: a thick woolly undercoat and a longer, sleeker top coat. We're hot!

I purr, therefore I am.

—Anonymous

What's your sign?

In Chinese astrology we have been assigned our own year. The Year of the Cat.

Now we cats just need a national holiday. You know, people buy us corny cards and cat ties that we'll never wear...

On the way to St. Ives,
I met a man with seven wives
Seven wives had seven kids
And seven kids had seven sacks
And seven sacks had seven cats
Wives, kids, cats, sacks
How many were on the way to St. Ives?

Answer... One: me!

—Anonymous

Here birdie, birdie, birdie....

Words from little friends...

"I like my cat cuz he knows how to hide. My dad bought him for me, but we couldn't tell my mommy for a couple of days cuz she didn't want me to have a cat. My cat stayed real quiet until my dad got the nerve to tell mommy. When my mommy saw my cat, she liked him and now they're good friends."

Kyle
Age: 5
Cat: "Fluffy"

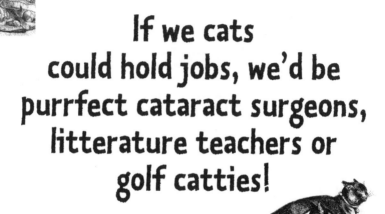

If we cats
could hold jobs, we'd be
purrfect cataract surgeons,
litterature teachers or
golf catties!

Funny SUPURRstition!

If a cat washes behind its ears, it will rain.
—English superstition

And you thought rain was caused from washing your car!

If man could be crossed
with a cat, it would
improve the man but
deteriorate the cat.

–Mark Twain

Cat Fact

Impawsible!

No, it's true! Cats are either left pawed or right pawed and some are ambidextrous.

But we're ALL paws when it comes to chasing those vermin!

A Funny Cat "tail"...

A cat named Mr. Cat ruled a local neighborhood and didn't like visitors. He went so far as biting the tires on any cars he didn't want around.

Moral: Don't tread on us cats!

Some of my fellow cats sure have been given some crazy names.

Eggroll, Gadget, Jamocha, Lapleach, Macaroni, Negatory, Perpetrator, Salami, Tutti Fruitti and Zero!

Excuse me...Did you forget we're sophisticated, elegant, smart, charming creatures?

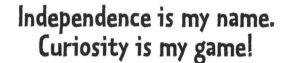

Independence is my name.
Curiosity is my game!

Did you hear the one about the
gambling tomcat that put
everything he had into the kitty?

Cat Fact

A sight to behold!

I'm called a Scandinavian Forest cat (Skogkatt). Who can resist my big emerald green eyes, expressive face and silky soft coat?

In spring I shed my magnificent winter under-coat and start to look entirely different (it's like owning two cats). As winter approaches, my mane begins to lengthen and soon I'm looking as spectacular as ever! Not that I'm bragging or anything...

FATAL ATTRACTION!

Everyone knows we cats love to play with string and rubber bands, but these cat "toys" can be fatal if ingested, so please take precautions.

I've heard we have nine lives, but I'd just as soon not test that theory...

What happened when
the cat ate a ball of yarn?
She had mittens!

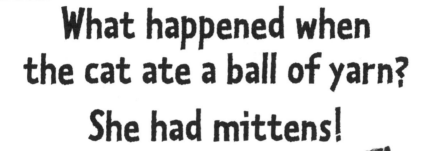

Tattoos are IN!

We cats don't mind carousing the neighborhood, but we don't like getting lost! So how about a tattoo? Tattoos cannot be lost or removed, they will protect us from theft and they will clearly identify us.

Plus, we can then join a rock band....

We Black cats get
a bad rap – we've always been
regarded as
omens of bad luck.

Gee, I don't remember having
any misfortunes!

Cat Fact

THE BETTER TO SEE YOU WITH!

We cats have a reflective layer in the back of our eyeball that works like a mirror on the retina to reflect the light back through the eye. This layer absorbs light 6 times more effectively than human eyes. Our pupils are more dilated at night and more of this reflective layer is visible, which gives our eyes their glowing effect.

You may have thought it was from our "glowing personalities"...

A cat sneezing is a good omen for everyone who hears it.

—Italian superstition

Catchoo!

Are CATS really WOMEN in disguise?

- We like having things our own way.
- We can be moody.
- We enjoy strokes and pampering.
- We're often misunderstood.
- We love interaction and play.
- We definitely love to snuggle.

BOO-BOOs

It is a myth that cats heal themselves by licking their wounds. In fact, licking can actually slow the healing process and create further damage to the wound.

And by the way, our pride is wounded when a cut comes from another cat...or worse yet, one of those "barking" creatures. So if we come home with a mark or two, the last thing we need is the third degree!

The Fountain of Youth!

We cats can help you reduce stress and add laughter to your life. Petting an animal is known to lower your heart rate, lower your blood pressure and brighten your mood.

So like what are you waiting for!

Catching some ZZZs

I'd really like to take a catnap

It's far more soothing than jazz, or hip-hop,
or even rap

The purrfect place is to curl up on your lap

I think I'll dream of you, my favorite chap

Jaguar, Lynx, Cougar

It took the folks at Cadillac about eighteen months to come up with the name Catera. The name combines Cat and Sahara, and research showed the name evoked sporty, sleek, agile and spirited (sounds just like us cats).

Flattery WILL get you everywhere!

What kind of shoes do cat burglars wear?
Hush Kitties!

Cat Fact

Owner BEWARE!

Human foods are often too rich for us cats to digest. One of the most dangerous human foods to give us is chocolate. Chocolate contains theobromine, which is extremely toxic to animals.

Oh how I wish this wasn't so!

Three reasons why I like my owner:

1) She gets impressed with little things I do

2) Love brings out the best in both of us

3) Without her, I would just wander

Cat Fact

Something to Stick Your Teeth Into!

Saber-toothed cats are among the most popular of Ice Age animals. Their canines were up to 7" long!

It would have been awful to be a mouse in those days!

Words from little friends...

"I like my cat because she meows two times. The first time she meows is to tell me she is hungry. The second time she meows is to tell me THANKS."

Madlyn
Age: 4
Cat: "Chelsea"

Cat Fact

SAVE THE CATS!

Some of the Big Cats, like the Jaguar, Snow Leopard and Tiger, are an endangered species. In the early 1900s, approximately 100,000 tigers existed in the wild. Today the estimated wild population is only between 5-7,000.

I can get through tight spaces
I can jump very high
I make a good spy
But how I wish I could fly!

Darn, birds always get away!

No, I don't dye my hair. It's natural!

Did you know the big cat we call the Black Panther is really a leopard? Its melanin (natural skin and hair pigments) produces a black fur in which the leopard's usual lighter coloring appears to have been dyed black.

But only our hairdressers know for sure...

Sing, sing! What shall I sing?
The cat's run away with the
pudding-bag string.

−*Anonymous Nursery Rhyme*

Words from little friends...

"My cat got stuck in a paper bag and went crazy running around the house with only his tail showing. He finally managed to free himself from the bag and found his favorite hiding spot, which he stayed in for a long time!"

Ryan
Age: 9
Cat: "Snicklefritz"

The smallest feline
is a masterpiece.

—Leonardo DaVinci

If it's not tied down
it's a cat toy!

—Anonymous

Cookie
the Sharpshooter

A cat named Cookie had a special trick of shooting rubber bands! He would hold the rubber band between his paw, pull back on the rubber band with his teeth, shoot it across the room, chase it down and do it over and over again.

Humm, with some practice, a cat could get its owner's attention pretty easily...

Cat Fact

A tailless cat?

The Manx cat can be born without a tail. Within the same litter there may be kittens born with a regular full tail, a short tail, a nubby style tail (known as a rumpy riser) or with no tail at all (referred to as rumpies).

No, this is not an old wives' "tail."

YA GOTTA HAVE SMARTS!

We cats don't fall for some of the things dogs do. Have you ever seen us pull a sled through the snow to win some stupid prize?

Catty Advertising?

-Reach Out and Touch Me...Please

-When You Care Enough To Own The Very Best

-Please Don't Squeeze the Kitty

Gone Fishin'

Although it may be true that most wild cats prefer land animals as their main food source, the Fishing Cat of Asia prefers to eat fish. It not only scoops the fish out of the water with its paw, but it can literally dive into the water and catch the fish with its mouth.

Oh no! We'll probably have to hear more stories about the one that got away!

Do you know peanut butter
works better than cheese in trapping a
mouse? On the other hand,
we cats work better than peanut butter
in trapping a mouse...

Mid life crisis is hell for cats.
It lasts a long time:
4th life, 5th life, 6th life!

I sniff, I claw, I paw

I pounce, I even hiss

But show me love

And I'll give you a purr and a kiss

Words from teenage friends...

"If my cat could talk, he would say, PRETTY PLEASE, LET ME IN YOUR ROOM! But I would first make him apologize for chewing (and ruining) my hair ribbons."

Lauren
Age: 15
Cat: "Tiger"

Dream Awakenings

Some dream experts claim that if you dream of domestic cats you are being warned to put aside self-pity and need to face up to challenges.

The perfect solution? Get a cat, or even two! We cats will take you out of your sandbox of self - pity and give you a jump on some mischievously good adventures and, uh, challenges.

Cat Fact

A tiger can consume as much as 80 lbs. of meat in one feeding. Holy Cow!

Gee, that is a cow!

Mouse and Garden's Tips for Cat Housekeeping

Sorry about all my cat hair, but you can easily remove it from surfaces by simply wearing a damp rubber glove and then swiping the area.

Also, I just love a clean and fresh smelling house, so you can keep my litter box fresh by adding 1 part baking soda then cover with 3 parts cat litter.

P.S.: Don't forget to let out the dog!

DO-RI-ME-OW!

I love to swing
I can even sing
Just give me string
And I'll do my thing!

Cat Fact

ALMOST FAMOUS

The most famous cat-like figure in Egyptian mythology was Bastet, the goddess of femininity and maternity. Her popularity made Egyptian women want to look like her, so they would line their eyes like the eyes depicted on Bastet to give them a more cat-like quality.

It's a good thing Bastet didn't have pink hair or something...

Words from teenage friends...

If you could ask your cat anything, what would it be?

"Exactly what do you do at night when you roam? Do you go to parties?"

Ryan
Age: 14
Cat: "Teaser"

Did you know that
"Sooty" is one of the most
popular cat names in the UK?

At least they didn't pick
"Snooty" or "Snotty"!

Cat Fact

See Spot Run!

The Ocicat and the Egyptian Mau are the only spotted domestic cats that most closely resemble the big cats of the wild. Although they have a wild animal look, their temperaments are anything but wild. They're very meek and mild. Meow.... (Unless you don't give them their own way!)

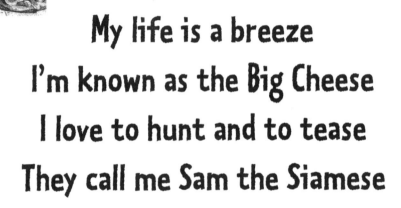

My life is a breeze
I'm known as the Big Cheese
I love to hunt and to tease
They call me Sam the Siamese

We cats need physical and intellectual stimulation. Although you can't take us out to the ball game, you can use simple items to entertain us.

Try tossing crumpled balls of paper for us. We also like to bat around walnuts (with their shells) over a hard surface or floor.

Wait until we get the hang of video games!

Cat Fact

Female cats can have as many as three litters every year.

Good thing we cats don't allow our children to come back home to live...

Who says
cats can't communicate?
Did you know our tails reflect our moods?

- If you see my tail erect and quivering, I'm happy and trying to say "Hi."

- If my tail is slightly raised and gently curved, I'm in a curious and snoopy mood.

- If it's moving side to side, I'm just a little confused.

- And, if my tail is low and fluffed out, I'm feelin' kind of scared (but don't tell anyone, we don't like being known as "scaredy cats").

We cats have been known
to possess psychic and E.S.P powers.
It must be our purring that does it.
It's our form of mantra.

Seems we always know where
our next meal is
coming from...

Did you know the Ford Thunderbird was almost named the Hep-Cat?

Did someone say bird?

Part of a cat's daily grooming/licking routine helps "waterproof" their coat. Licking stimulates the skin glands (which then creates a secretion that keeps the fur weatherproof).

In other words, we cats have a natural London Fog® jacket! And you thought it was just because we enjoy fur balls...

Cat Fact

Tuna Talk

Although we cats might love the human variety of fresh tuna, we should eat it sparingly and only mixed with our regular cat food. If consumed on a regular basis, cats can develop a vitamin B1 deficiency (due to an enzyme in tuna that can destroy a cat's B1 supply).

I guess I'll have to skip "Tuna Saute à la Chiffonade Under Glass" tonight...

Cat's favorite newspaper: The Scratching Post!

WARNING! Toxic Plants!

Lilies can be extremely toxic and dangerous if we cats ingest them. In fact, numerous indoor and outdoor plants can make us very sick. Please check with your vet if you are uncertain.

Feel free to leave catnip handy, however...

I need to watch my figure!

One of the heaviest domestic cats on record weighed 47 lbs! Humm. I bet he could just look at a mouse and scare him to death!

SIAMESE:
The Pavarotti's
of the cat world!

Cat Laws-

- Thou shalt take frequent naps and leave little fur balls wherever it lies.

- Thou shalt sleep with thy owner and make them as uncomfortable as possible.

- Thou shalt seek out any flat lying rug in which to mangle into a ball.

- Thou shalt seek out the best furniture pieces to scratch beyond repair.

Cat Laws—
(continued)

- Thou shalt only like the most expensive cat food and refuse all others.

- Thou shalt sit on thy owner's lap whenever he starts to read a book or newspaper.

- Thou shalt interrupt all phone conversations.

- Thou shalt, above all else, pretend to be interested in its owner— especially when hungry.

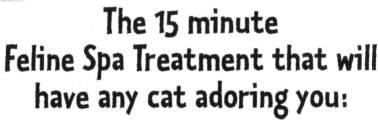

The 15 minute
Feline Spa Treatment that will
have any cat adoring you:

5 minutes of brushing and combing

5 minutes of massage

5 minutes of play

Cat Fact

FACT or FICTION...

Myth: All cats should drink milk.

Fact: Most veterinarians recommend we cats avoid milk. Our digestive system does not digest milk well and may cause diarrhea, leading to future health problems.

Shoot! I sure like that stuff. Why is everything I like bad for me?

Have you listened to KATT radio lately?

Sunshine On My Backside

Thank God I'm Country Cat

Benny & the Cats

Ain't No Owner Like the One I've Got

Scratch Fever

Tuna on My Mind

It makes me feel like purrin'

Kittens remind us
to laugh at ourselves,
to find time to play,
to simply love life

Cat Fact

It's SUPER CAT!

I'm sure you know that most of us domestic cats can jump many times as high as our height. Even better, our feline friend, the African Serval, can catch birds flying as much as 6 feet from the ground.

We need to be in the NBA!

Cats in the Bag!

We cats enjoy unusual and interesting sounds, which is one of the reasons we enjoy playing with a plain paper bag. We love the sounds they make from scrunching, crumpling and pouncing on them! We also like to move them around, sit in them, sleep in them and hide in them.

Guess we're the original bag ladies...

Are you an Ailurophile?
That's a fancy word for cat lover.
(YEAH!) An Ailurophobe is one who
hates or fears cats. (BOO, HISS!)

How do you pronounce those
words anyway?

CAT HEALERS

Cats do not need to go to medical school. We seem to be natural healers. In fact, in the Middle Ages some Europeans believed that cats could help cure people who were insane. In Japan, some people believe cats can cure melancholia and epilepsy.

When exactly can we expect payment?

Cat Fact

What a PURRformance!

The first major cat shows were held in England in 1871 and in America in 1895. Hundreds of cat shows are now held annually throughout the world. They're fun, and they're a great way for cat fanciers to learn more about pedigreed cats and the numerous breeds. If you attend, however, please don't touch! You might muss my hair!

Have you
ever wondered what a cat's
idea of retirement is?

Some authorities
believe cats were domesticated
about 5000 years ago in Egypt.

Cats, domesticated?
Isn't that an oxymoron?

Cat Fact

CAT STATs

- No one knows the exact domestic cat population in the U.S. However, estimates range anywhere from 30 to 60 million.

- More cats are owned than dogs.

- More than half are stray/feral cats

Wow, I knew I was popular but that's a lot of CATS!

Let's play
Hide and Seek!

We cats like unusual places. Perhaps you'll find me curled up in a big old shoe... or on top of the refrigerator... or nestled behind a bunch of books... or maybe right in front of your nose, lying on top of the television.

Let's face it, I wrote the book on making myself at home.

Here is a list of my feline friends that require very little grooming and brushing:

- Abyssinian
- American Shorthair
- Bombay
- British Shorthair
- Cornish Rex
- Devon Rex
- Siamese
- Sphynx

We're the NO MUSS, NO FUSS gang!

Cat Fact

Birman cats have lovely white paws, and some people think they look like they're wearing white gloves. Their legend is that a white cat rested her paws on the body of her beloved deceased human companion (a pious monk). His soul then passed into her, turning her fur to gold. However, her paws remained snow white!

Now that's the white glove treatment!

Catnet.com

We cats love surfin' the net—we get to play with a mouse all day!

Cat Fact

Need a new "DO"?

The LaPerm cat doesn't need a perm! The LaPerm has naturally curly and wavy hair. Sometimes it will even have ringlet-type curls. Interestingly, however, some LaPerm kittens can be born hairless or will go entirely bald before developing their beautiful locks.

Menopaws = A time
when older female cats are plagued
with hot flashes, insomnia, and
rage over simply nothing.

There is no snooze button
on a cat who wants breakfast.

—Anonymous

Cat Fact

Standard Cat Features!

Whiskers are like radar that help us cats roam in the dark without bumping into anything! Whiskers also indicate our mood (watch out when they're pulled back; come snuggle when they're forward).

But our whisker's primary use is judging distance. Our whiskers are about the width of our bodies (kind of a built-in ruler). If we stick our head in and out of an opening, we're probably judging the width of the opening to see if we can fit into it. Pretty handy, I'd say!

You have now learned to see

That cats are much like you and me

And other people whom we find

Possessed of various types of mind

Other Titles By Great Quotations

301 Ways to Stay Young At Heart
African-American Wisdom
A Lifetime of Love
A Light Heart Lives Long
A Servant's Heart
A Teacher Is Better Than Two books
A Touch of Friendship
Angle-grams
As A Cat Thinketh
Astrology for Cats
Astrology for Dogs
Can We Talk
Celebrating Women
Chicken Soup
Chocoholic Reasonettes
Daddy & Me
Erasing My Sanity
Fantastic Father, Dependable Dad
Golden Years, Golden Words
Graduation Is Just The Beginning
Grandma, I Love You
Happiness Is Found Along The Way
High Anxieties
Hooked on Golf

I Didn't Do it
Ignorance Is Bliss
I'm Not Over the Hill
Inspirations
Interior Design for Idiots
Let's Talk Decorating
Life's Lessons
Life's Simple Pleasures
Looking for Mr. Right
Midwest Wisdom
Mother, I Love You
Motivating Quotes,
    for Motivated People
Mommy & Me
Mrs. Murphy's Laws
Mrs. Webster's Dictionary
My Daughter,
    My Special Friend
Only A Sister
Parenting 101
Pink Power
Reflections
Romantic Rhapsody
Social Disgraces

Someone Pleeease pull
    The Fire Alarm!
Stress or Sanity
TeenAge of Insanity
Thanks From The Heart
The ABC's of Parenting
The Be-Attitudes
The Cornerstone of Success
The Lemonade Handbook
The Mother Load
The Other Species
The Rose Mystique
The Secrets in Your face
The Secrets in Your Name
The Secret Language of men
The Secret Language of
    Women
The Sports Page
Things You'll Learn...
Wedding Wonders
Word From The Coach
Working Woman's World

Great Quotations, Inc.

8102 Lemont Road,
#300, Woodridge, IL 60517
Phone: 630-390-3580   Fax: 630-390-3585